I0476259

Blogging Brilliance

How To Make A Bundle On Your Blog

Brad Jones

Copyright © 2015 HRD Publishing

All rights reserved.

ISBN-13: 978-1515146742
ISBN-10: 151514674X

CONTENTS

INTRODUCTION

Have you ever considered going against the norm of your everyday life in search of something more fulfilling?

Do you love writing? Do you want to spread a wealth of knowledge? Do you like helping people find solutions to their problems?

If this is the case then maybe you are someone who should consider making freelance blogging your new career move.

While it can take some work setting up a Blog and get the money rolling in, blogging can be a great opportunity to work to your own schedule, focus on something you're passionate about and make a decent living all at the same time.

Let's get one thing straight, Blogging is not a "get rich quick" scheme. It's a venture for those who are ready to dedicate themselves to working hard and building up an online reputation in a particular niche, and to begin with, for little financial return. However, those that stick to it are greatly rewarded in the end by working within a subject they're interested in and they can make a very nice income from it. All of the hard work will pay off if you just keep your mind to it. Before you read this book, you should ask yourself if you're prepared to put the work in to achieve this.

The world of freelance blogging has been growing significantly over the last five to ten years and it is not slowing down any time soon. If you love to write, have a particular niche area that you already know a lot about (cooking, gaming, cars, and just about any hobby you can think of, you can blog about!) then this could be a great opportunity for you to lend your knowledge to others while making a profit from it!

This book is going to cover everything from creating a Blog, getting an audience, and show you how to earn a full time wage blogging. This is the chance you have been waiting for, to break free from the harsh 9-5 world for good and spend your time working on a passion for a living.

Read on and take the action steps at the end of each chapter to become a successful blogger!

SO WHAT IS BLOGGING AND HOW CAN I MAKE IT MY CAREER?

What is a blog?

The simple definition of a blog is a web log, where a person will write posts about a specific topic.

For example, there are blogs about cooking that give you helpful tips and awesome recipes. There are blogs about gaming that will review the newest video games with a full list of pros, cons, important cheats or hacks, news on upcoming games and more.

Blogs like these are highly successful because they focus themselves in a particular niche where they can thrive. If you try to stretch your blog through too many topics, your readers will have a hard time following and will most likely lose interest.

While most blogs are focused on a certain hobby or area of interest, some people make their blogs more personal, with tales of their life and their experiences. These blogs are usually more for someone that is looking to blog as a hobby rather than a career but even these blogs can become highly successful when maintained properly.

If you, like so many others, have a few different areas of interest and cannot pick one single thing to blog about, consider making more than one. Having multiple blogs can help you cover multiple areas of interest and reach many different readers in an effective manner. As a starting point, I suggest setting up one Blog for now and learning the process before committing to too much early on.

How do Blogs make Money?

Bloggers make money in a number of different ways, depending on the niche they are in, what their skill set may be, their knowledge (and willingness!) to incorporate different revenue generating schemes into their blog.

One of the widest known ways for a blogger to make money on their website is to have paid advertising on your site through Google AdSense or similar. This means that when people click on the advert, you get a small payment. Depending on the product, the reader might need to place an order on the item, before you receive payment for it. You'll also get a very small payment for just having the advert on your page too, regardless if anyone clicks on it or not. Google AdSense is great for blogs with relatively high traffic on a regular basis. The more readers, the more potential you have for people to click on the ads or view them.

Some bloggers like to guest post on other blogs. This is not only a great way to make money but also a great way to bring traffic to your blog. Many big name blogs will not only pay you for the article or post you provide for them, but they will also give you a chance to provide a short bio and link to your own blog at the bottom of the post.

Choose a blog that has a subject similar to your own site or that you can write a post that relates even in a small way to you own content. This way, the people reading your post on that blog will want to read more from you and then follow the link in your bio and become a follower of your own site.

There are many other income generating ideas such as affiliate marketing, creating membership subscriptions, selling products and services to name a few. I'll be going into more detail on each of these subjects later on in the book. Each one has the potential to generate a lot of money, and when combined they can create a significant income – enough to quit your 9-5 job and work for yourself!

Gaining loyal readers is a key to starting a career as a blogger!

Every successful blog has one thing in common – a faithful core group of readers. They are there every day, week or month depending on how often new posts go up, looking for new content!

If you really love to write, then you may be able to use your blog in even more ways to make money. People offer writing services directly from their blog as well as self-publish e-books on Amazon Kindle and then promote them on their blog. This is actually a rather common form of income for many bloggers.

(Check out the "Be a Freelance Blogger" site, "Leaving Work Behind" or "Reboot Authentic" for an example of a blogger who makes a living with nothing but blogging!)

There are many routes you can take when you are looking into become a professional freelance blogger and it all depends on your interests and individual goals. It can be a long process but it is a highly rewarding one for those who are dedicated.

How Much Can I Really Make?

This really depends on a number of factors. Consider how much time and care you put into creating your blog, whether your blog is a sub-domain or self-hosted, if you are writing only for your own blog or others and how much you really want it! All these things will roll out to decide whether or not you are going to be a successful blogger.

That is not to say that there are no successful blogs with a sub-domain rather than a self-hosted one. It also isn't to say that people who write only on their blogs make any more or less than those who guest post often on other blogs. The very last item, how much you really want it, is the one that will make the biggest difference of all.

You have to really go for it, you cannot just create a blog and expect it to magically start making money. You have to sink time and love into your writing, your blog and people will see that! They will see a dedicated, hardworking person and they will want to work with you or continue to read all your posts! This is how you are going to become a successful blogger!

Actions from this chapter:

• Write down at least three potential niches you could Blog about. Which idea are you most passionate about? Could this area develop products, services (like coaching) from you or other people? Choose the one that appeals most to you.

• Determine your goals and write them down: consider hosting situations, how often to post, think about revenue streams you may use, what are your monetary goals for the next six months to a year and beyond?

HOW TO START YOUR OWN BLOG

Now that we have a general understanding of what a blog is, let's move onto the burning question: How do I start my own blog?

Starting a blog is relatively simple to do and the cost can vary. Depending on what you intend to use your blog for, what expectations you have of your blog in the long run and how much you can invest into your start-up will be determining factors in how you approach this.

Low Cost Blog Options for Beginners

There are many free options for people who are looking to just get their feet wet in the blogging community. Websites like WordPress.com and Blogger.com (formerly blogspot.com) are both brilliant and free options for starting your blog!

Both websites offer a free blog with a sub domain (www.example.wordpress.com or www.example.blogger.com) which can be a great way to go if you are completely new to blogging. If you want to look just a little more professional, you can always buy a domain name and still use their free package. (Which is great if you already own a website domain!)

These free packages come with a free blog, at least a few different pages you can add to your blog as well as basic customization features. This helps you to bring a personal touch to your blog.

These low cost options are perfect for beginners. You can sample the life of a Blogger, completely free of charge, and see if it's something you want to take more seriously in the future. It's a low risk option that provides exposure and you can still earn money on them. The downside to these options are the lack of flexibility in comparison to owning your own domain. It's not that they are inflexible. They just don't have as many restrictions (eg. website design, layout and advertising) that a self-hosted domain has. I started out using a sub-domain Blog, and I would recommend them for people starting out.

Mid-Range Cost Blog Options

If you know for sure you want to be blogging for quite a while and you don't want to waste any time getting a professional look, but do not have a ton of start-up money then there is an option for you.

There are some web hosting sites such as BlueHost.com that allow you to create a professional website with your own domain and paid for space on the internet (more than you get with the free option) as well as better customization, all for a low monthly fee depending on the package you choose.

When you are looking to go for a very professional feel right from the get-go and you have some capital to start with, then this is could be a great way to go. There are many hosting sites with a plug-in for WordPress or similar blogging software to help you build your blog to exactly what you are looking for. You have far more room for customization and freedom with this option.

In It For The Long-haul and Ready To Invest

There are also options to start your blog and have all your services paid for up to a year or two in advanced! Depending on the hosting provider you choose and the amount of space and customization you want to achieve, the price range can be anywhere upwards of $100.

WordPress.com offers an intermediate package at an annual cost of $99, which allows you a domain name, nearly unlimited pages and customization possibilities. This is probably one of the best offers out there, since WordPress will help with all of your Search Engine Optimization (SEO - which we will talk about soon), which is a major advantage they have over competitors such as Blogger.com.

Choosing to pay for your blogging package all at once is actually less expensive in the long run than choosing a month-to-month 'Mid-Range' cost option in most cases above. The only problem is (and we understand) not everyone can just let go of $100 or more all at once. If you can afford it though, this will save you money and hassle (no worry of forgetting a payment!).

Only you can decide which package is right for you. Is there an option that stands out to you based on the information above? If not, why not start with the 'Low Cost' platform, and work your way up.

Setting Up Your Blog

Now that you have chosen what package option works best for you it is time to actually set up your blog. The first thing you need to do is choose a niche topic and title for your blog. This is how your blog will be remembered by your readers and one of the most important decisions that you make when starting out.

When it comes to your domain name, try to be original and creative, but at the same time keep it simple. For example, you do not want people to remember that your website is called "Jesse's Graphics" but not remember that the domain name is spelled "Jesse's Graphix". Try to leave out numbers, avoid odd spellings and keep it relatively short. This will ensure your readers can find you again, without needing Google.

What websites and blog's do you regularly visit? If you like a particular website name, think of the reasons why? Is it funny, original, relevant to the niche or all three? How can you implement a similar approach?

Once you've decided on a niche and a name, you can start looking through the theme options for your blogs design. There are hundreds to choose from and the more you paid for your blog hosting the more options you are likely to have for it.

Choose a design that is simple to navigate and easy on the eyes. You don't want to make it hard to read or look at for a long period of time.

After all, you want people to stay on your blog and read all your content.

Choosing the right font is also important, you want to stick to something simple that will be standard on any computer. Some fonts are specific to Mac, Microsoft or even only computers of people who downloaded the same font package as you.

After you have designed your blog it is time to think about content. Not only do you want to have new posts going up regularly, but you need to have a few pages on your site as well. Pages are the section headers at the top of the site. Some common options include an "About" page, a "Contact" page and maybe a "Services" page if you are selling your blogging services.

Creating an Engaging About Page

Your about page is really a way for your reader to get to know you. They want to know who you are, what your passions are and why you are blogging. The more you want to tell the better in most cases.

Start off with an introduction about yourself. Some bloggers opt for a third person introduction, which looks something like this:

"James started out as a writer for his local high school paper when his dream of being a journalist began. Since then he has received a degree in Journalism from BLANK University, as well as traveled internationally to work as a freelance reporter writing for papers and online publications around the world on major news events.

Years of travel and experience in other countries has brought him to creating THIS BLOGS NAME, which is intended to help people traveling abroad to know what to expect, things they may not think to pack and much more."

You can put as much or as little detail as you feel is necessary. Be creative, captivate your reader with your story. Let them see that you are human! Better yet, if you are looking for the most personal approach of blogging, why not try writing from your own perspective.

An example of writing from your own point of view:

"When I was in high school I started writing for the school newspaper. Ever since then I knew I wanted to be a big time journalist. I got my degree in Journalism from BLANK University in 2005 and since then have traveled all over the globe to write for several major publications both online and offline.

I started this blog because I feel my years of traveling has left me with knowledge to share about traveling abroad. I want to help people prepare, know what to expect, what they may need and more, before they ever step foot on a plane."

Find a couple of blogs that you really like, that are already successful and look to them for examples of a brilliant and effective about page. Everyone's writing style is a little bit different, so don't try to exactly copy them, but instead pull ideas from all of your favorites to create your unique style.

Creating Consistent Content is Key

You have already chosen a niche for your blog, a title and created your "about" page. Now, unless you are adding more pages (services offered, contact, etc.), you have the basics and it's time to start working on your content!

There are a few big things here that you want to make sure that you remember when writing your content:

- Use proper spelling and grammar

- Don't be too formal or too informal either

- Post often – more content means more traffic

If you follow these three key steps, you are well on your way to being a professional blogger. The importance of these tips cannot be underestimated. People will not take you seriously if you are talking like you are in a chat room using slang and text speak. Yet, you don't want to bore them to death by sounding like textbook either. Finding a nice balance between information and entertainment is a tried and tested route to success.

Creating content that is relevant to your niche and making sure that you format it well is so very important. Think about articles you read online, Top 5, Top 10, 5 Things you shouldn't…, 7 Tips for…

These examples are great headline starters and they will help you later on when you are working on SEO (Search Engine Optimization).

Make your posts conversational and easy to read, but also make sure that all your information is accurate. If you are using statistics or facts in your post, link back to the source of the information. This will help inform people what you say is the truth and not made up simply to bring traffic to your blog.

Once you have a few posts up, you are on your way, but don't stop there. Now you need to update your blog regularly. Whether it is once a day, two or three times a week or what, just make sure you stay consistent. Once you have built up a small following of readers, you will see your audience grow faster when you are consistently updating with new content.

They will share it with their friends and their friends with their own, this is when it really snowballs. It may take a little time to reach this point, but the more quality content you deliver on a consistent basis, the more likely you'll be finding success blogging.

Actions from this chapter:

- Choose a hosting package to suit your needs.

- Create a unique name for your niche and write a great 'about page'.

- Make a goal of writing a set number of posts a week or a month that you can consistently keep to.

- Start writing your first high quality content post to bring in new readers.

BRINGING TRAFFIC TO YOUR BLOG

Your blog is now set up, with a beautiful design, a creative title and a killer 'about page'. You have even written a couple of blog posts, staying on topic and with a great headline. Now, how are you supposed to get people to find you?

This is where SEO comes into play. It's time to cover how you are going bump your site up in the Google rankings.

Google is the world's number one search engine by a huge margin and you've probably used it countless times. Now it's time to learn how to make Google work for you.

Simply put, Google uses an algorithm to decide where your website or blog is going to rank among the thousands of others. This is determined by a number of different factors, meaning there is a lot you can do to affect your SEO ranking.

First things first, generally, self-hosted blogs are going to rank higher than sub-domain ones. The main reason for this is you are seen by Google as someone who is serious about your website, business and brand when you are willing to spend the money on that original domain name.

Keywords are Excellent SEO

Second, you need to use keywords as best as you can. You are probably given space to ad tags to your post – these will show up under the post on your home page. These tags can be anything relevant to you and your blog or even that post in particular.

Once you have your tags set up, use keywords in your content as well! Using a few sets of keywords often throughout the post (and better yet in the title and any headings) is a great way to bring up your rankings with each and every post you write.

The way Google treats keywords has changed some over the years and is undoubtedly going to change again someday, but the main idea is consistent. Think of what people would type into Google when searching for something like your blog.

If you have a blog all about cooking tips and tricks, then use key word phrases such as: Cooking tips, Cooking tricks, tips for cooking, and so on. If you can generalize it even more each post then do it! If your newest post is 5 Great Meals You Can Freeze, then use keywords like, freezer meals, freezing leftovers, meals you can freeze and so on.

Use Social Media for SEO

If you really want to get the word out about your site one of the fastest, cheapest and most effective ways to go would be using social media. Make a separate page dedicated to your blog on Facebook, Twitter, Instagram and even LinkedIn (you can use your personal pages too – the suggestion of a separate page is to keep your personal and professional life apart). Then whenever you post on your blog, send out a little blurb about the post and a link on each site.

This is not only a great way to make sure people know about your new blog and know it has been updated, but it also helps a lot with Google's algorithm as it factors in your social media presence when determining where you are going to rank on the list!

Do yourself a favor though and during those initial months of set up when you don't have a lot of followers, do not get sucked into buying "Likes" and "Followers" on your social media to promote your blog. This is not only cheating but those followers are all fake and you can actually end up losing some or all of the followers that you obtain them in this way.

Besides, even though your social media following is going to be monitored by Google and having more followers can boost your ranks, you need to remember they need to be active followers. Someone who not only liked your page but also shares and comments on the content. Google is smarter than you think and you cannot fool them with these fake followers!

Even though it might take longer, sharing your pages with your friends first and letting word get around that way is better for your blog and brand in the long run. Don't hurt your business by doing something like faking followers. (Which at least on Facebook is now against their TOS).

Consider YouTube as well as Social Media

Now that you have your social media pages for Twitter, Facebook, Instagram, Pinterest or Google+ (or better yet, all of them) it is time to move on. Have you ever considered making videos for YouTube?

Whether you get up in front of the camera yourself, use animation or turn a simple PowerPoint presentation into a video, you can get great exposure by using YouTube.

A huge proportion of the human population prefer visual communication. Some may not be avid readers of your blog, but will always watch your videos on YouTube. Although these people may not be your initial target audience, they are a sure fire way to build your audience further than just writing.

It can be a great way to introduce people to who you are. Create videos that are relevant to your blog but make sure it's unique and original! Don't just read your old blog posts.

By doing this you are opening yourself up to a world of new followers. Link your videos to your blog and vice versa. Even dedicate a link in your main navigation bar to your YouTube Channel.

Another great tactic to promote not only your blog but all of your social media, is to use a call to action at the end of each and every video. You've probably heard something like this before, "If you liked this video, subscribe to this channel and follow us on Facebook and Twitter for more epic stuff from BRAND NAME HERE."

YouTube can also help to increase revenue streams by bringing more people to your Blog for Google AdSense, products and services, but you can also earn money from your YouTube videos due to the adverts they place on them. Similarly to AdSense, the more subscribers you have to your YouTube Channel, and the more views your individual video clips have, the higher your potential to earn money. Once you've made a video your work is done. You'll continue to earn royalties on it as long as people view it.

Promoting Your Blog via Forum Posting

There are many people who use this method of promoting their blog, business or brand. Forum posting is great if you are a very social person or an expert in your field. This gives you a chance to answer questions, ask questions all while linking back to your blog when it is relevant to your post. A lot of people use their signatures in order to link to their blog so that it is seen after each and every post they make.

Here are a few forum posting tips to keep in mind:

- Be active.

- Post relevant and helpful content.

- Follow forum rules!

- Use links wisely.

By following these few tips, you can become an active and respected member of any forum. If you do not follow these tips and you post everywhere you can, filling your posts with backlinks to your blog, you will be regarded as a SPAMMER. No one wants to be known as a spammer, your online reputation is at stake and your forum accounts are likely to be deleted.

Being active is probably the most simple, but most difficult thing to do on a forum. Try to make at least two or three posts per day, whether they are in old topics, recent topics or a whole new thread you started. If you start the thread, try to be active with the people commenting on it. This is a great way to build up your reputation on the forum as people will get to know you and trust you the more you post helpful and relevant content.

Which is tip number two from above, always, always, always post relevant and helpful content! People will not respect you if you simply go around linking to your blog or website when you have nothing beneficial to say. Forums are a give and take process, you must give them helpful and quality posts and in turn people are much more likely to click through to your site.

This actually goes right along with the very last tip which was to use links wisely. Do not only link to your own blog. Find other members on the forum who are known for posting helpful content and link to them. It feels great to help others out, and they may extend the same courtesy to you! Also, instead of filling up your posts with links, put them in your signature and in your profile. This way, once people have decided you are trustworthy on the forum they can click through whenever they like.

Actions from this chapter:

- Use strong keywords.

- Social Media is your best tool. Sign up to at least three separate social media accounts.

- Use YouTube to bring more traffic and appeal to a whole second community with videos. Record 3-5 videos and see what response you get from it.

Forums are a great place to meet people and socialize while advertising your blog if you are active. Leave a comment every day, and try to help at least three people out by linking in their sites.

RUNNING A GREAT BLOG

Creating a great blog is not only about the content and building a following. One of the biggest parts of running a successful blog is that you love what you are doing. If you don't, then why are you doing it anyway? The most successful blogs are run by people who are motivated to write and one of the easiest ways to boost enthusiasm is to write about things you're passionate about.

Successful bloggers take their hobby to the next level, giving advice or teaching others about a subject. If you're able to write about a topic you're interested in, it won't feel like 'work', and you'll be able to offer more help to people as you have a genuine interest in the area. Giving yourself and your blog a purpose will help to show people that you are not just in it for the money, and in turn you will increase your earning potential.

Many blogs offer advice to people just starting out in an industry – for example there are many blogs that are just about blogging. These blogs will often have some of the best tips for new bloggers and they are a great place to keep in mind for guest posting later on when you are more experienced and established as a blogger.

Think about all the websites you visit on a regular basis and think about what they do. What is their blog or website all about? What is their target audience? Is that the same audience that you are trying to reach?

These are great questions to ask yourself. The fact that you bought this book would suggest that you might already follow other blogs and perhaps even comment on their posts regularly. Why? What is it about the blog that stands out for you?

If you are trying to decide on your blog topic still – or maybe a way to make your topic more specific, this is a great way to get ideas. Look at blogs and websites from your same niche and see what they are posting.

People are attracted to a few things on the internet more than others.

For example, Do-It-Yourself projects, solutions to problems and the latest in the entertainment industry are all things that people commonly search for on the internet.

How can you use this information to bring more people to your own blog?

Within your niche, try to find an angle that will allow you to bring a solution to a common problem through a series of content. Package your posts into small series. For example, have five posts that are all centered on a theme, or upcoming holiday.

Plan out your posts to avoid repetition. If you covered a topic two years ago and your view on it since has changed, then sure, go for it and write a new post. On the other hand, the rest of your content needs to be unique, fresh, and something that your readers are yet to see.

No matter what you are blogging about, remember that you need to keep a fresh look on things. Do not bore your readers with information spun off of old articles already out there on the web. There's a possibility your readers have already read that work. You want to give your readers a reason for going onto your blog. If you found an article interesting, how can you take it to another level? Can you dig into the subject in more detail or could you use your blog as a live diary account of your experience. For example a day-to-day account of the latest diet, training routine or online course you've taken.

There is nothing wrong with taking inspiration from other great blogs. Try to take that motivation to a new place or share your experience of using a product, service or method.

Actions from this chapter:

• Stay passionate – your readers will notice and your blog will be successful.

• Look to blogs that are already successful for ideas to improve your own blog. Don't copy anyone, but pull inspiration from these sites. Make a list of the things you like about the blogs you visit. Are there any trends?

• Write down some ideas of how your blog can stand out from the others in your niche.

• Always consider ways to help or inform your reader in your posts as well as entertain. It will help you build a loyal following.

THE REAL MONEY MAKERS OF BLOGGING

When you decide to take up blogging you are opened up to a world of opportunities for making money. I've briefly mentioned in the previous chapters some of the ways you can make money - freelance blogging, advertising, e-books and offering products. We're now going to explore how you can make money with your blog in a little more detail.

Mailing Lists are Powerful Tools

A mailing list is created when people subscribe to your blog – they sign up with their e-mail so that they will receive an e-mail update when you have put a new post up. This e-mail list is one of your most powerful money making tools.

There are many different ways you can utilize your mailing list:

- Promoting products or services you have for sale

- Affiliate marketing

- Exclusive offers for subscribers

To use your mailing list to the best of your capabilities, you need to realize what a truly amazing tool it is to keep in your arsenal. The people who have subscribed to your blog and allowed you to send e-mails directly to them are people you already know are interested in what you have to say. These people are already looking to you for information, a service or something of that sort.

If you have decided to go the freelancing route and are using your blog to promote your sales, then try something like offering a special deal to anyone that responds to an e-mail. Make it a one-time offer, or a limited time offer. Make sure you have a call to action that just screams, "You need this and you need it at this great price now."

26

Also, remember, freelancing can be any sort of service you provide for a fee. Even consulting or life coaching can be considered freelancing. Just make sure that you provide an exceptional service for the money you are asking. There really is truth to the statement "Under promise and over deliver."

The same idea works for you if you're selling products like e-books. Give your loyal readers a reason to stay loyal readers – give them early access to these e-books, or give them a code to get a discount whenever possible. Sometimes, even offering one of your books for free is a great way to bring them in to buy more. After all, if you are good at what you do they will want more and more. It's not about getting a smaller cut on one job or one project, it's about creating a lasting relationship between you and your trusted reader and buyer.

Affiliate marketing works in a very similar way. When you choose the route of affiliate marketing you are getting a small cut of someone else's product or service when the customer is directed to them by you. If at all possible, try to arrange a deal where you readers will get a discount on this item or service when they purchase it through you. This will be a great promotion technique that will vastly benefit you and the person offering the product or service.

When you offer any of these things, talk it up and make it known that it's a great, once-in-a-lifetime sort of deal. This way your readers will feel special, you'll save them money and help them by directing them to a product that they'll find value in. They took the time to follow you and you are giving them great deals in return. What's not to like there?

I would recommend that you only suggest products/services that you've used and valued to your readers. You will run the risk of losing readers if you recommend products that you haven't used and turn out to be a waste of money for them. Not to mention the fact that it isn't ethical to do so.

A popular site to use for Affiliate Marketing is ClickBank.com. They have a huge amount of products to recommend and sell on your blog for all sorts of niches.

If your blog supports a non-profit organization, you can even use mailing lists to kindly let people know that you are supplying a certain type of work or product for free but donations are greatly appreciated. Include a link to your donation page and an exceptional thank you to those who donate. If possible – set up a system where the bigger the donation, the better the freebie. People will be glad to help a great cause and will be even happier when they get something great in return for that kindness.

Create a Members-Only Site Addition

One of the best examples of a blog that uses a members-only site addition is Make a Living Writing (.com)'s Freelance Writer's Den. This website is an additional site that is accessed by members who pay to be a part of the site. The site offers exclusive training, access to job boards and so much more.

Of course, this member's only area is not free, this is where the money making comes in. People pay either monthly or annually for a subscription or membership to this particular site. Here's the deal breaker though – you have to make it worth their money to join!

While you should always offer some sort of freebie content to all of your readers, make sure there is exclusive content that would not be available to them otherwise. This is really a great way to make money – and consistent money at that – from your blog.

By offering them a wealth of knowledge that goes beyond your original site or blog is an excellent opportunity to take when you are working online. It will give you a little more security in your income, while giving your members a place to get better information in a single, convenient place.

There are many examples of member only subscription sites out there now. Some sites offer a free trial period. If you're able to find any free trials, especially if it's in your niche, sign up to it and experience what they offer. This will give you an idea of how you could incorporate the same thing into your blog.

Of course, you don't have to wait for free trial periods. A lot of the subscription memberships allow you to join for as long as you like. You could pay for one month, experience the service, and cancel the membership after you have some ideas. Either way, if you're planning on creating a membership only section on your blog, I recommend you experiencing one beforehand.

Advertising Does Pay

Top Ways to Monetize Advertisements:

- Google AdSense and AdWords (CPC/PPC)

- Sponsors

- RSS

One of the most common ways to make money with your blog is through advertising. There are several different types of advertisements that will bring in money but one of the biggest is cost-per-click advertisements like Google AdSense.

Basically, when you sign up with Google AdSense you will display advertisements on your site. When people click those advertisements, you will get paid a small fee per click. Is this an extremely lucrative money making option? Yes, absolutely! Though as with anything else, it is going to take time to get it going to its full potential.

Google AdSense is not the only cost-per-click company around, but it is one of the most well-known and trusted companies.

If you are looking to have an advertisement yourself to boost your sites traffic and therefore boost your own cost-per-click campaign, then you should consider using Google AdWords. This is different from AdSense in that you are the one creating an ad that Google will bring up under certain keywords in a pay-per-click campaign.

The great part about Google AdWords is that when you are only going to have to pay for it when someone clicks your link! You can set your budget too, which is a great feature. This way when your budget is reached, your link will no longer be advertised and you won't be spending any more money on it.

Aside from CPC and PPC, there are many other ways to get your blog out there, such as getting a sponsorship for your blog. Having sponsors for your blog is similar to pay-per-click, but instead they are paying your directly for promotion of their business. If you have a relatively large following you can even consider sending out offers to people who you would want to have sponsoring on your blog.

Setting up a page for sponsorship is also a great way bring in potential sponsors. They will see the page link in your navigation bar, get curious and click. If you have everything clearly detailed and outlined for them – how much it costs for what kinds of ads on your site, along with an "order now" feature (like you get with PayPal) you are likely to get at least a few spur-of-the-moment sponsors.

Another possible route is RSS or Rich Site Summary. This is an online program that allows readers to follow many different websites in one convenient place.

When you set your blog up to be RSS available, people will automatically see all your new posts in their RSS feed. It is similar to that of a Facebook feed, but instead of pages that were "liked" you are shown the websites you visit most often, every time they put up new content! What better way is there to make sure your readers never miss the next big thing you post?

These RSS programs will automatically supply your readers with your newest posts and a link to your blog. This increases your Google ranking and makes sure that readers know right away about your new post. This is like instant advertising as far as bringing your site more traffic goes.

Affiliate Links are a Great

If you like shopping online, then you know how much other people must love shopping online. If you're anything like me, you'll search for a product on Google or Amazon and once you've selected an item, you'll pay close attention to the customer reviews. It's amazing how influential feedback is. If an item has over fifty reviews and all of which are five star, you feel reassured to make the purchase. If an item has five reviews, four of which are negative and suggest not buying the item, how might that impact your decision to buy?

Generally speaking, most people care what other people think. There are of course exceptions to the rule. For example, some people will not respond to feedback, whilst others will make their decisions solely based on the opinions of others.

Once your blog has built a number of regular readers, it would be fair to suggest that those people find value in your writing. There's a good chance that they'll respect your opinion, especially when it's relevant to your niche. This puts you in a powerful position.

You could now review products that are relevant to your niche topic and receive a small commission from every sale your recommendation makes. How awesome would that be?

This is the reality when you use Affiliate programs such as Amazon Associates and ClickBank.

With programs like these, you are given an affiliate link, which when someone clicks it, will take them directly to the product. When a reader of your blog clicks through this link, Amazon or similar sites will recognize that they were linked from you. If this reader purchases an item, after being directed to it by you, you will receive a small commission.

This might not seem like a lot of money and it might not be at first. But once your readers have built up a trust with you, they will be more likely to buy on your recommendations. As sales go up, your commission check goes up.

You help your readers find value in a product, and get paid for doing it. Not a bad job!

This is one of the best ways to create a passive income with your blog. Even old posts with links in them will still bring in the money months and months later. Think about how much your income will grow as you review more and more products.

Even if you only write about one product a week, that is still 52 products a year that you are promoting. That link will continue to bring you revenue every single time someone reads your article, clicks the link and buys a product!

For people who are newer to the world of affiliate linking, it is best to start up with a company like Amazon. Amazon Associates is a simple affiliate program with a very clear outline of everything.

Once you are a little more comfortable with how affiliate linking works, you should consider moving to ClickBank; which is one of the number one affiliate marketing programs for bloggers and website owners everywhere.

Actions from this chapter:

• Consider all the different options for income streams and which will work best for your blog.

• If possible, use multiple income streams in order to get the most out of your blog. Which ones work best for you and your blog? Don't limit yourself.

Register accounts with ClickBank and Amazon Associates. Find at least three items on each platform that you could recommend on your blog.

IS BLOGGING RIGHT FOR YOU?

We have covered all of the most important aspects of creating a blog and starting a blogging career. Hopefully this e-book has given you the confidence to go for your dreams, reach for the stars and start a blog that could change your life.

At this point you have been shown how to start your blog, you have some idea of the pricing options, how to run a successful blog, how to drive traffic to your blog and how to keep those readers on your site.

With this information at hand you should be prepared to start your blogging adventure. You already know it is going to be a slow moving process at first – but also that you will be better off for it in the long run. After all, wouldn't you much rather work really hard for a few years and enjoy the benefits for the rest of your life, rather than working moderately hard or for your entire life?

When you learn to create passive income streams through advertising, affiliate links, membership fees, merchandise, and more, you can spend your time enjoying life and less working it away.

If this sounds like you, and if this sounds like the life you want to live, then below are some of the best resources for your new entrepreneurial adventure as a blogger.

Hosting Sites

www.wordpress.com

www.blogger.com

www.hostgator.com

www.bluehost.com

All of the above sites are used by very well-known bloggers. While some may be better than others, it all depends on the needs of you and your blog individually. Look through all the options and consider the pros and cons to make a decision on hosting. There are many more sites than this, but these are all highly recommended by freelance bloggers.

Blogging Tips and Resources

www.problogger.net

www.problogger.com

www.beafreelanceblogger.com

www.leavingworkbehind.com

www.rebootauthentic.com

www.makealivingwriting.com

The sites listed here are all blogs that are about blogging. They come with wonderful tips by professional bloggers. These people have been running one or more successful blog for quite some time now and want to share what they have learned with you. Some of them even offer free e-books when you subscribe to their blog. All of the content is worth it – and subscribing means that you will always have quick access to their latest posts. This will help you keep informed as trends in the blogging world change.

CPC Programs

- Google AdSense

- Bidvertiser

- Media.net

- InfoLink Ads

- Chitika Ads

These programs were listed.com on www.safetricks.com as the top five out of their top 11 best CPC Programs.

PPC Programs

- Google AdWords

- Yahoo! Bing Network

- Buy Sell Ads

- AdRoll

- 7Search

Google AdWords is one of the most well-known PPC programs out right now to boost traffic to your site with PPC. If you want to reach more markets by going through with more than one PPC campaign, then www.ppchero.com suggested these alternatives to Google AdWords that are mentioned above.

Affiliate Programs

- Amazon Associates

- ClickBank

- Commission Junction

- LinkShare

- ShareASale

While Amazon associates was mentioned earlier in the e-book and are probably the easiest affiliate marketing program to set up, there are many alternatives out there. I mentioned ClickBank in the book, and I've listed a few more to get you started. Look through all of them and make a decision based on which one you believe your site will profit most from.

SUMMARY

Blogging is an excellent career opportunity for any entrepreneur or aspiring entrepreneur. If you are already freelancing then you can enhance your business by promoting it with your blog. It's also very rewarding. You get to spend your time writing about subjects you're passionate about, whilst connecting with great people all over the world, who enjoy the same things you do.

If you know you have the passion and dedication it takes to stick with your blog, you will benefit from the end results. Especially since the results will never end! When you optimize your blog with the right income streams, you can eventually make a very decent living while working very few hours.

This would allow you to spend more time doing things you love, like spending time with your family, going to the movies with a friend or relaxing on a beach. All of those are possible when you have your blog making money for you!

It is definitely not a means to get rich quick, but in time you'll be handsomely rewarded. With hard work and perseverance your blog will bring you a bigger return than you could have imagined.

If you want to become financially independent in the future, you need to be prepared to work hard now. Set your goals prior to starting a blog, write powerful, emotive reasons to why you want to achieve those goals, and take steps every day to get closer to them. When the going gets tough, look back at your goals and remember 'why' you are doing all of this. If your goal and the reason behind the goal aren't strong enough, you're much more likely to quit before you reach the level of success you want. Just remember, you will be reaping the rewards of all that hard work for years and years to come if you just stick to your goals and keep moving forward.

Anyone can start a blog and add content regularly, but someone who with determination, drive and passion can turn that hobby into a never ending stream of income.

I wish you all the very best of luck with your blogging journey!

OTHER BOOKS BY BRAD JONES

Fiverr Freedom: From Your First Gig To Making A Fortune On Fiverr

Ebay Excellence: Making Easy Money The Ebay Way

Flawless Freelance Writing: How To Make A Fortune Freelance Writing